RUBANK EDUCATIONAL LIBRARY No. 90

RUBANK INTERMEDIATE Method

FRENCH HORN

E♭ ALTO or MELLOPHONE

J. E. SKORNICKA and R. ERDMAN

A FOLLOW UP COURSE FOR INDIVIDUAL OR LIKE-INSTRUMENT CLASS INSTRUCTION

RUBANK, INC.®

Hal Leonard Publishing Corporation

7777 West Bluemound Road P.O. Box 13819 Milwaukee, WI 53213

T0071560

ESSENTIAL PRINCIPLES

of

Good Instrumental Performance

GOOD TONE is necessary in order that one's playing be pleasing to the listener as well as the player. Good tone can be produced only when the instrument is in good playing condition, equipped with the correct type of mouthpiece and played with the correct embouchure.

INTONATION: When two successive tones of different pitch are produced, it is necessary that each tone be in tune with the other, relative to the interval being played.

TUNE: The player must develop and train his ear so that a difference of pitch can be distinguished when playing with others.

NOTE VALUES: The player must develop a rhythmic sense so as to give proper value to tones as represented by the written notes.

BREATHING AND PHRASING: Each is usually dependent on the other. Since teachers of wind instruments differ on the methods of breathing, no special method is advocated, but it soon becomes evident to all players that in order to get good musical phrasing, it is necessary to breathe properly and in the proper places of a composition. It will be to the pupil's advantage to spend much time and effort on this phase of playing and take seriously all suggestions given by the teacher.

EXPRESSION MARKS: Expression marks in music are considered just as important as punctuation in prose and poetry. Good phrasing is the performance of music that has been properly punctuated. Expression marks put character into a mass of notes and if properly observed, will produce satisfying musical effects.

RELAXATION AND PROPER POSITION OF BODY AND HANDS: Whether playing in standing or sitting position, it is necessary that the body be erect and relaxed. Relaxation is the secret to the accomplishment of success in many other professions and trades. The arms must be relaxed, the elbows away from the body and the hands assuming a restful position on the instrument.

SUFFICIENT TIME FOR PRACTICE: Since different pupils require different types and lengths of practice periods, the objective that every pupil should establish is: "I will master the assigned task whether it takes 1/2 or 2 hours." The accomplishment of a task is far more important than the time that it consumes.

PROPER CARE OF THE INSTRUMENT: Carelessness in the handling of an instrument is the most prevalent handicap to the progress of young players. No pupil can expect to produce good results if the instrument is in poor playing condition. The instrument must be handled carefully and when a disorder is discovered, have it remedied immediately. Constant attention as to the condition of an instrument will pay dividends in the end.

MENTAL ATTITUDE OF TEACHER AND PUPIL: In order that the musical results be satisfactory, both the pupil and teacher must be interested in their task, and must have a perfect understanding of what that task is. The teacher must understand the learning capacities of the pupil so that the pupil in turn will get the type and amount of instruction that he will understand and be able to master.

J. E. S.

Fingering Chart

NATURAL TONES

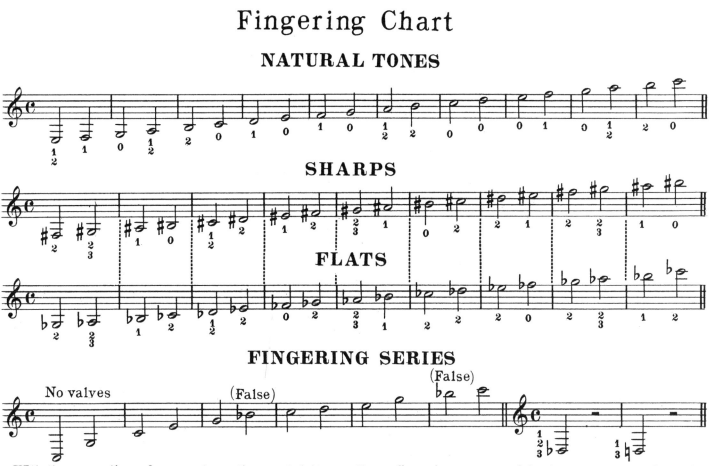

SHARPS

FLATS

FINGERING SERIES

No valves   (False)   (False)

With the exception of one or two other pedal tones, these fingering produce false tones and are not usable.

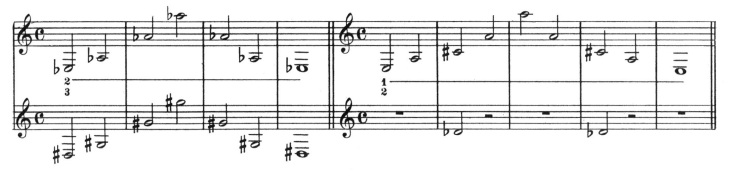

Pedal Bb

Pedal A#

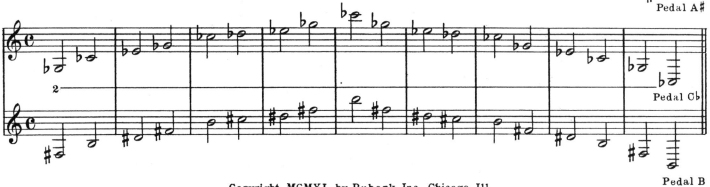

Pedal Cb

Pedal B

PREPARATORY STUDIES

1. Have the instrument in good mechanical condition, namely, valves well moistened or oiled and slides properly lubricated.

2. One of the important essentials in performance of music is a sound rhythmic conception. When this conception is established, correct playing will result at sight.

3. In playing the succeeding studies, special attention must be placed on the proper adjustment of the embouchure. Not all players are able to attain the same type of embouchure, but the one that produces the best and easiest results must be discovered by both the teacher and pupil.

4. Rhythms in this lesson are fundamental, and their mastery will make playing fluent and comprehensive.

NOTE AND REST VALUES

Rests are just as important as the notes. In this lesson and all succeeding lessons, make sure that proper values of both rests and notes are carefully observed.

Since the range of the Mellophone and E♭ Alto are more limited than that of the French Horn, small notes will appear throughout the book, making such passages playable for all three. In such cases, the Mellophone and E♭ Alto will play the small notes.

When two sets of fingerings appear, the lower is for French Horn and the upper for Mellophone and E♭ Alto. When only one fingering is used, it is the same for all three.

MARKS OF EXPRESSION AND THEIR USE

PIANISSIMO	*pp*	Very soft	FORTISSIMO	*ff*	Very loud
PIANO	*p*	Soft	FORTE	*f*	Loud
MEZZO PIANO	*mp*	Medium soft	MEZZO FORTE	*mf*	Medium loud (Normal tone)

A tone produced on a brass instrument should be played at the same level of volume unless otherwise indicated. In the following studies parallel lines will indicate that type of tone. The distance between the parallel lines will indicate the volume of tone to be played.

p ═══════ *pp* ═══════ *mp* ═══════ *mf* ═══════ *f* ═══════ *ff* ═══════

DAILY LONG TONE STUDIES

SLURRED LONG TONES

These studies are important in obtaining flexibility by opening lips and relaxing pressure on low tones as well as closing lips and increasing pressure on the high tones.

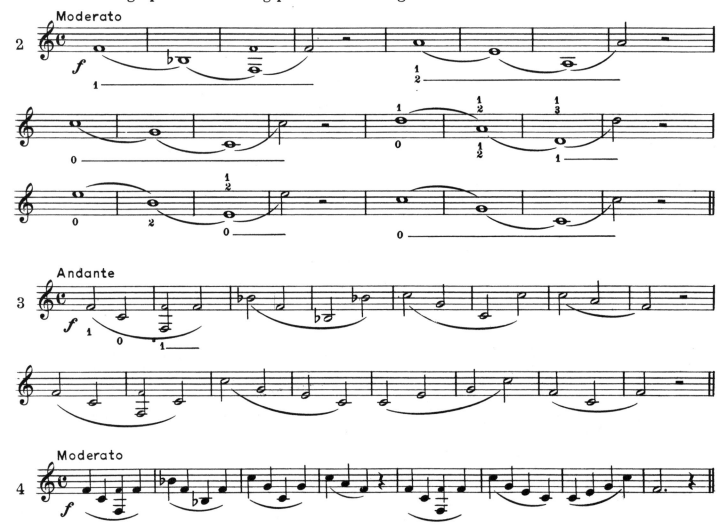

6

STUDIES IN EXPRESSION
Sound Graduations

Crescendo (cresc.) Gradually louder.   Decrescendo (decresc.) or Diminuendo (dim.) Gradually softer.

In playing a crescendo or a diminuendo the pitch of the tone should not change.   It is a common fault of especially young players, to play flat when playing loud and sharp when playing softly.

In order to play the sound graduations or nuances correctly, it is necessary that the quality of the tone is not affected, but retain its rich and mellow fullness. ONLY THE VOLUME SHOULD CHANGE.

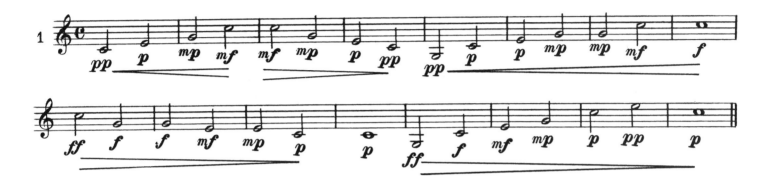

When a note is followed by one or more shorter notes, the shorter notes are played with one half the vol-ume of the longer note. There are exceptions to this rule, but it is a good policy to learn to play all phrases as mentioned, since the majority of all music played in this way will be properly performed.   Players interested in the fundamentals of solo playing will be greatly aided by adhering to this principle.

Using exercises 1 and 2 as patterns, write in the various volumes required in the playing of the suc-ceeding song. This will acquaint the player thoroughly with the sound graduations required in the pro-per performance of solos and songs.

BLUE BELLS OF SCOTLAND

Folk Song

The expression marks as indicated in all music are actually a part of that music and should be ridgidly adhered to. Correct reading of notes is only one phase of musical performance; expression marks are a means of making music out of a mass of notes.

LEGATO ETUDES

ETUDE EXPRESSIVO

Accents (Rinforzando)

The rinforzando or accent (>), placed over or under a note indicates that more weight or strength of tone should be used. It puts a stress or emphasis on important tones of a measure or sequence.

WALTZ

FORWARD MARCH

ACCENT ETUDE

Serenade

J.E.S.

Andante

Staccato Studies

STACCATO ETUDE

MINUET

STACCATO INTERVAL STUDY

Transposition

Although many different types of transpositions are found in the playing of classics and most of the symphonies, the common one that the school musician encounters is the playing of E♭ Alto parts on the F Horn. It is presupposed that at this stage of Horn playing, transposition will have been introduced and used, however, a brief review is made here for the convenience of those who have not been familiarized with it.

This transposition consists of playing the E♭ part a whole step lower. If all of the keys have been studied and learned, it is most satisfactory to transpose in keys as follows: When the signature of the E♭ part is in flats, add two flats to the signature and play in that key, and if the prevailing signature is in sharps, subtract two sharps and play in that key.

THERE IS NO SUBSTITUTE FOR THE THOROUGH KNOWLEDGE OF ALL KEYS.

In order to obtain sufficient experience on the above transposition, it is suggested that preceding lessons in this book be reviewed by supposing that they are written for the E♭ Horn and transpose them on the F Horn. When the student has comfortably mastered one transposition through the knowledge of keys, all other transpositions will be relatively easy.

Technical Staccato Etudes

POLKA

Allegro

1 *simile*

Also transpose as E♭ part.

COUNTRY DANCE

J.E.S.

Allegro

2 *simile*

MALA POLKA

Allegro

sempre staccato

sempre staccato

D.C.

Scale and Chord Studies

F Major Studies

F MAJOR CHORD

F MAJOR SCALE

SCALE ETUDE

INTERVAL STUDY

D MINOR STUDIES

D MINOR SCALE *(Harmonic)*   *(Melodic)*

ETUDE IN D MINOR

Syncopation

1

2

₵ SYNCOPATION

3

2/4 SYNCOPATION ETUDE

4

6/8 Rhythm

RAPID TONGUING ETUDE

ETUDE for TONGUING and SLURRING

Triplet Studies

MELODY IN 6/8 TIME

MELODY IN 2/4 TIME

MELODY IN 12/8 TIME

TECHNICAL ETUDE

B♭ Major Studies

B♭ MAJOR CHORD

1

B♭ MAJOR SCALE

2

STACCATO ETUDE

Allegro

3

simile

LEGATO ETUDE

Moderato

4

G MINOR SCALE *(Harmonic)*

5

G MINOR SCALE *(Melodic)*

6

Lip Slurs and Pedal Tones

When two successive notes of different pitch are slurred without the change of valves, it is called a Lip Slur. Lip slur exercises will appear in many of the succeeding lessons and are intended for the purpose of strengthening the lips, lip muscles as well as other face muscles. At first the muscles of the face will tire rather quickly, but with daily practice will become strong and flexible, thus making the playing cleaner and easier. Do not hinder the flexibility of the lips by pressing them too tightly against the mouthpiece. Daily practice of lip slurs is the procedure followed by all good professional brass instrument players.

Chromatic Studies

CROMATIC SCALE

ENHARMONIC CHART

CHROMATIC ETUDE

LEGATO CHROMATIC ETUDE

Familiar sharps and flats.

New and not familiar sharps and flats.

Allegro

Allegro

Dotted Eighth Note Studies

DOTTED EIGHTH NOTE STUDY

Moderato

JOY TO THE WORLD

Moderato

OH TANNENBAUM

Andante

Chord and Scale Studies

D MAJOR CHORD

D MAJOR SCALE

LEGATO SCALE STUDY

Moderato

mf *cresc.* *dim.* *cresc.*

mf *cresc.* *dim.*

Allegro

B MINOR SCALE (*Harmonic*)

B MINOR SCALE (*Melodic*)

MELODY IN B MINOR

Andante

f

E♭ Major Studies

E♭ MAJOR CHORD

1

2

E♭ MAJOR SCALE STUDY

Moderato

3

LIP SLUR STUDIES

4

MELODY

Andante

5

C Minor Studies

Eb MAJOR SCALE

1

C MINOR SCALE (*Harmonic*)　　　　　　　(*Melodic*)

2

C MINOR ETUDE

Andante

3

DUET IN C MINOR

J. E. S.

Moderato

4

A Major Studies

A MAJOR CHORD

1

A MAJOR SCALE

2

LEGATO ETUDE

Moderato

3

STACCATO ETUDE

Allegro

4

HEAVENLY HOSTS ARE SINGING

Andante

Traditional

5

Technical Studies

DANCE No.1

DANCE No.2

DUET IN A

LIP SLURS

Rhythmic Development

MELODY IN 6/8 AND 3/4 TIME. No.1

No. 2

RELATIONSHIP OF 6/8 AND 3/8 TIME

ALLEGRO IN 3/8

Syncopation Etudes

FOLK SONG

Bohemian

Articulation Studies

ALLEGRO

MODERATO

A♭ Major Studies

Crusaders' Hymn

Traditional

GAVOTTE IN A♭

J. E. S.

Chromatic Studies

2/4 TIME

6/8 TIME

CHROMATIC ETUDE

omit for Mel. and Eb Alto

Articulation Etude

LEGATO DUET

J. E. S.

Scale Studies

Scale Studies

Folk Song

German

FOLK SONG

German

Austrian National Hymn

HAYDN

RUSSIAN NATIONAL HYMN

Trio in E Flat

R.W.E.

Grace Notes

There are two kinds of Grace notes, short and long. The long grace note acquires half the value of the note that it accompanies, and is seldom used, since it is easy to write out two notes of equal length. The short grace note is the one that is commonly used and will be used in succeeding studies.

In addition to the single grace notes there are double and triple grace notes, but these are usually written out and played on or before the beat. As to which one it shall be is usually determined by the type of music being performed.

SINGLE GRACE NOTES

DOUBLE AND TRIPLE GRACE NOTES

GRACE NOTE ETUDE

Scale Studies

Folk Song

Poland

Sharpshooter's March

METALO

Allegro

Muting and Stopping

For the player whose desire it is to understand the complete resources of the French Horn, it is necessary to obtain the best possible muting effect. At the outset, there should be no confusing of the terms "muting" and "stopping".

"Muting" is produced by placing the palm of the hand across the opening of the bell, thus lowering the pitch of the instrument one half step and somewhat muffling the tone. This process is rather uncertain, since "playing out of tune" will result if the ear is uncertain. However, when short passages or phrases in the middle register call for muted horn or "gedämft" this method of playing may be employed without disasterous results. It is possible to purchase transposing or non-transposing mutes but the fact still remains that a good horn player uses the hand methods exclusively.

"Stopping" the horn is used particularly in obtaining distant or echo effects and for passages such as are used in "Til Eulenspiegel" by Strauss. The hand is straightened and pushed into the bell of the instrument, thus shortening the tubing and causing the pitch to rise one half step by virtue of over-blowing the tones. Thus, a thin brassy tone is obtained and all notes so indicated (+) must be transposed one half step lower.

Muting lowers the pitch of the horn one half step therefore it is necessary to read muted passages one step higher than written.

Stopping raises the pitch of the horn one half step and therefore it is necessary to read stopped passages one half step lower than written.

Bass Clef

A versatile horn player should have such command of the instrument that he will easily cover the entire range in a most flexible manner. While this implies a finely trained embouchre, it also means fast and accurate reading. Although most horn passages are written in the treble clef, there are many symphonic passages, solo parts and an increasing number of lower quartet parts being written in the bass clef to facilitate reading. Most passages consistently below F (leger line) are written in bass notation.

Bass note equivalents

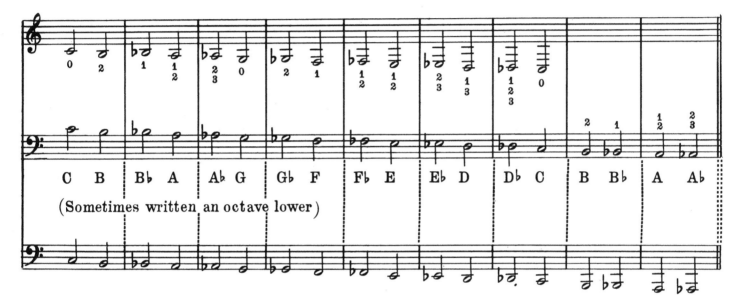

Most bass clef parts now written give the notation as actually sounding so that the succeeding exercises will be played accordingly.

Drink To Me Only With Thine Eyes

Arr. by R.W.E.

From "Freischütz"
OVERTURE

Adagio

WEBER

From
THE PRELUDES

LISZT

Andante maestoso

4th Part for
French Horns only

Lip and Finger Trills

A trill is produced by alternating the given or written tone and the next scale tone above in rapid succession. In a finger trill, if the given or written tone to be trilled is E and the key being played is C major, the scale tone above will be F natural. If however, the key being played is G major, the next scale tone will be F♯. In the first instance, the trill will alternate between E and F natural and in the second instance between E and F♯.

The number of trill notes is not always the same, this depends on the kind of music being played and the type of a trill that may be most desirable or appropriate. In long trills, it is customary to begin the trill slowly and accelerate to the end of the tone, thus giving the music individuality.

Short trill without closing tone.   Long trill with closing tone added.

At times it is necessary to alter the pitch of tone above the written tone in the trill or the closing tone. This is done by indicating a sharp or flat above or below the trill sign. Such alterations are designed to help fit the key in which they appear.

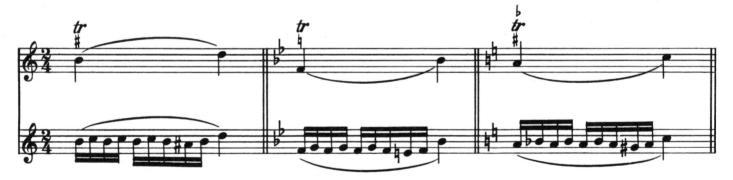

Lip trills are more common in horn passages than finger trills, since the overtones are used so frequently. Thus common fingerings on adjacent tones are easily trilled by slight variations of lip pressure. Such trills are always whole steps.

48